Tormey Hogan Architects.
September 2009.
01- 6629243

CITY HOUSES

BETA-PLUS

CITY HOUSES
originally published in Dutch and French
STADSWONINGEN / MAISONS DE VILLE

PUBLISHER
BETA-PLUS sa
Termuninck 3
7850 Enghien
Belgium
Tel : +32 (0)2 395 90 20
Fax : +32 (0)2 395 90 21
Website: www.betaplus.com
E-mail: betaplus@skynet.be

PHOTOGRAPHY
Jo Pauwels a.o. (photography credits p.200)

LAYOUT
POLYDEM sprl
Nathalie Binart

TRANSLATION
TxT-IBIS (Dutch to French)
Yvonne Lim and Serena Narain (French to English)

January 2006
ISBN: 907-721-359-7

NEXT

A contemporary city
house transformed by
architect Joel Claisse.

LEFT

A work of interior designer Filip Vanryckeghem (iXtra).

CONTENTS

PREFACE

Living in the city offers a series of advantages: public transport, proximity to amenities, schools and work places, museums, sports centres, restaurants, etc. The city attracts an increasing number of young people, as well as the elders who return after having lived in the countryside or quiet suburbs for decades.

This book presents a series of recently renovated and remodelled urban residences: majestic master houses that are restored to their original glory, as well as contemporary island houses, exclusive villas, and new apartments, lofts and penthouses.

A similarity lies in this range of diversified works: the inspirations of architects, interior designers and the residents into a spatial unity, serenity and quality of life that are reflected in the structure of each house, and in the selection of materials and colours.

This publication serves a source of inspiration for those who currently reside in the city, or are aspiring to purchase or rent a house to soak in the glorious sights and sounds of city life.

NEXT
The work of interior
designer Nathalie
Van Reeth.

LEFT
A work of Obumex.

CHAPTER 1

CONTEMPORARY CITY HOUSES

THE REFLECTION OF A MODERN WAY OF LIFE

A family with four children decided to settle in a semi-detached house in Brussels and engaged the services of architect Baudouin Courtens.

The dwelling was completely renovated three years ago and is still in very good condition. However, Courtens understands that the house did not suit family's way of life. Consequently, instead of some required interior arrangements, it is a total recasting of the garden level and the beautiful upper floor that Courtens proposes to his clients.

The result is a bright and comfortable house, a custom-made craft, a reflection of a modern way of life and the dynamics of the house owner.

P.16-17

The definite options from the start by Courtens include: re-establishing the contact with the garden, introducing lights all over the house and creating a connection between the garden level and the upper floor.

P.18-21

On the garden level, all the partitions are removed to create a large open space overlooking the garden, where the kitchen and dining area are located.

The living room occupies the whole width of the façade facing the garden. It is structured by horizontal lines from the open chimney and the bench.

P.22-23

The oak and steel kitchen is open yet made intimate by a large sliding panel in front of the central island. A huge mirror that enlarges the space is placed on the wall above the cooking stove.

P.24-27

A very beautiful collection of contemporary art lends the place a discreet air of sobriety, and also determines the choice of materials and colours. The range is intentionally reduced in order to create a unity in the project.

All the furniture is designed by Courtens and created by Vendredi under the supervision of the company Durce.

A COLLECTION OF CONTEMPORARY ART

Architect Pascal Van der Kelen has restored an urban dwelling from the 17th Century within the Flemish Brabant. Serene and contemporary, the interior is emphasised by artworks selected by artistic advisers A. and J. Gordts.

P.28-29

The façade is entirely restored with a historical base.

At the garden side, unique window panels at the back façade facing south are elongated to the ground to allow ample light into the house. Similarly, the kitchen is given a large corner window that offers a magnificent view diagonally into the garden.

P.30-31

On the ground floor, the dwelling is conceived like a presbytery with a central corridor connecting the road and the garden.

In the corner salon, a full-height book cabinet was constructed according to the drawings of Pascal Van Der Kelen. The "Surrogates" by Allan McCollum is placed opposite the cabinet. The photo opposite is the work of Robert Mangold.

The strong symmetrical character of the central entry hall (with the reflection of the double door leading to the dining room) is accentuated by the architect due to the symmetrical layout of the square table and the dresser. The furniture of the dining room is made of Macassar ebony and enamel glass. A 1986 work by Ettore Spaletti is displayed in the background.

The existing staircase is tinted in a darker colour.

The kitchen is constructed in bleached timber and brushed stainless steel. The kitchen chairs are constructed according to the drawings of Mallet-Stevens.

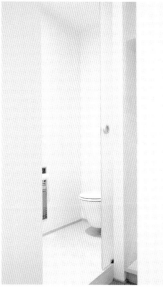

P.34-37

On the second storey, four small bedrooms have been transformed into a large suite. The rooms in a row offer a splendid perspective view and allow a full review of the façade in front. Acid-treated glass panels separate the bedroom, the two dressing rooms and the bathroom. The bathroom is entirely finished in Greece sandstone. The shower floor and the wall are finished in grey/green bottle glass mosaic. The dressing cabinet is finished in a lacquered material and sanded glass.

P.38-39

The bedroom is finished in bleached oak panels.

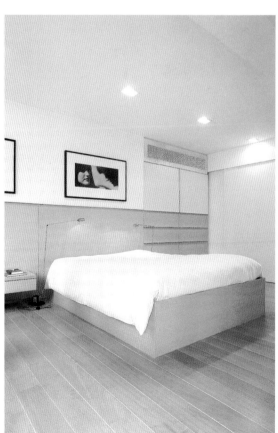

PURE BEAUTY

Interior designer from Brussels, Francois Marcq, has transformed a large space into a secondary residence:
a project out of the ordinary and one of a pure and natural beauty.

THE PROFOUND TRANSFORMATION
OF AN OLD CITY HOUSE

Acquired in 2002 by its current owners, this 20th Century house has been thoroughly transformed by architect Christine von der Becke.

The objective is to attain a sense of equilibrium between austere and modern tendencies concerning space, light, opening, etc.

P.48-49
The architect has transformed the backspaces on the ground floor and on the second storey.

LEFT & P.52-53
The kitchen and the corner dining area form a whole, offering spectacular views of the terrace and garden. The parquet is entirely restored and oiled. The kitchen cabinets are custom-made in MDF and tinted oak. The chairs are from Ethnicraft, the lighting is from Constanzia and the concealed spotlights are from Modular.

LEFT
The marble of the entry hall is polished and the timber works are painted white.

P.54-55

The structures have to be modified in order to open up the spaces to introduce lights: the corridor has disappeared to create space. The landing is enlarged and gives access to the children's bedrooms and to the bathrooms.

P.56-57

The intermediate room, transformed into a dressing area, is reconnected to the room to accentuate the opening. The lighting colour procures a warm and sober ambience. The dressing cabinet is finished in painted MDF and tinted oak. The sliding door is in tinted oak.

ART AND DESIGN IN A CONTEMPORARY
URBAN DWELLING

Interior designer Patric Deknock has designed a villa in a small town in the west of Flanders: a work that perfectly illustrates his predilection for Italian design and his love of modern art.

P.58-59

The kitchen floor is finished in cast Graniglia. Six dining chairs from Zanotta are placed around the ancient oak table. Above the table is a light from F.A. The countertop is finished in stainless steel and the cabinets are in transparent laminates. The glass cabinet is from Dorma (Manet system). Artworks are from De Paris.

A Zanotta sofa in red velvet and a Doma armchair in white leather surround a coffee table that is designed by Patric Deknock. Stools from Promemoria.

Similary designed by Patric Deknock, the table is made of ebony wood. The chairs are from Promemoria and the light on the ceiling is from Driade. The huge lithograph is a work of Folon. The walls have received a whitewashed paint finish.

LEFT
View of the music room from the hall.

The floor, shower, bathtub and the washbasins are covered with imitation white marble. The integrated cabinets and cupboards are in transparent laminates.

In the hall, two works by Bayard surround a glass door.

CHAPTER II

CLASSICAL INSPIRATION

SUBTLE EQUILIBRIUM

Situated in the heart of nature yet near to city centre: this exceptional house offers the best of both worlds.

The house was originally constructed just before the Second World War. It has undergone major restructuring by architect Philippe Cuylits in the 1980s. Fifteen years later, the owners engaged Joel Claisse who did not conserve anything in terms of important works except for the staircase, dining room, living room and the open chimney. Volumes and living spaces were notably enlarged; the impression felt is that of lighting, spaces and perfectly balanced lines that seem timeless yet extremely current at the same time: a truly pleasant house that reflects calmness and serenity.

LEFT
The entry door of the grand façade at the side is reopened and light floods the ground and second floors. Four small windows are also added in.

P.67-69
A double living space is added to the principal cubic building: to the left of the photo on P.67 is an open terrace, to the right is the dining room with large windows that provide a beautiful view of the garden. The furniture in the dining room is from Christian Liaigre.

The owners are true art lovers. The works of Sugimoto, Antony Gormley and Roni Horn are found in this home.

LEFT
The staircase, lacquered in grey, is one of the few elements that remain from the ancient residence.

ABOVE

The more formal dining
room consists of furniture
by Philippe Hurel.

P.76 Bottom and
On this Page
The kitchen, in sand and
Bordeaux tints, is
constructed by Obumex
in collaboration with
architect Joel Claisse.

P.78-81

The general use of earth colours and natural materials create an intimate and serene atmosphere, a reflection of a subtle balance.

P.82-83

The bathroom is a creation of Axel Verhoustraeten. An artwork of Riva Boren hangs above the bathtub.

A BRUSSELS STYLE MASTER HOUSE

In great respect of the authentic characteristics and in close collaboration with the owner of the house, an 1880 Brussels style master house was renovated by Jos Reynders Décor and its interior design done by decorator Helena van den Driessche.

The unique advantages of this type of master house - like the very high ceilings, the tall doors and windows, the balance structure, layout of the rooms or the detailed finishings, are exploited in an optimal manner.

P.84-85

The design is typical of master houses at the end of 19th Century, complete with high ceilings, high doors and windows to allow the penetration of light in an optimal manner and to procure a strong sense of space.

The floor strips on the ground floor are laid like an open book. Behind the sofa, on the left of the photo, a French window is added to allow the view of the hall from the living room: a solution adapted from a small staircase core, typical of ancient master houses.

LEFT
The lampshades are custom-made by Histoire de Famille (Fabienne Verbesselt).

The original elements (chimney, double door in beveled glass, ornaments, etc.) are conserved as much as possible.

P.88-89

Curtains are not used in order to allow the optimal penetration of light.

P.90-91

The open kitchen is conceived by Fahrenheit. There was a separation wall before where the island countertop is now.

In order to give the impression that these materials have always been there, the designer has chosen to use oak and old glass.

P.92-95

A contemporary classical decoration of the bedroom with seagrass carpet and a canopy bed.

P.96-101

The owners wanted a connection between the master bedroom and the bathroom on the mezzanine, so a portion of the existing dressing area is utilised in the creation of an access to the principal bathroom. The bedroom, bathroom and the dressing constitute the only unique huge room in a loft style. It is for that the window was enlarged and a staircase added.

A HISTORICAL CONSERVATION

The site of Filature Gevaert formed a part of Thomas Gevaert's life since his birth. During his architectural studies, he inherited one of the three workers quarters situated in the Gevaertsdreef, which is now classified as a conserved house.

The classified front façade has to be conserved but the layout of the rooms is radically modified. The two upper storeys with high ceilings are replaced by three levels with standard ceiling heights to help increase the total floor area.

Since the levels no longer correspond to the window openings of the original façade, the floors are isolated from the front façade where a staircase is installed.

The living rooms are situated on the upper floor to create an impression of a larger space. The corner salon extends from the front façade to the back and is prolonged even more by a terrace as an external space, an opening that assures a visual connection instead of physical one with the garden.

LEFT
By placing the staircase along the front façade, different zones each with its very own function are envisaged parallel to this.

P.104-105
Staircase, kitchen and corner dining areas are situated on the third storey. The absence of walls and the staircase as a decorative element connects the storeys, in a way, as a vertical loft.

P.106-107

The bedroom, bathroom and the garden are found on the ground floor.

A CONTEMPORARY TOUCH

Interior designer Nathalie Van Reeth has transformed a typical semi-detached house dated end of the 19th century to a both pleasant and contemporary whole.

The objective was to open up the spaces and introduce light into the house, thus the three rooms that follow one another and the centre staircase core result in a narrower room in the centre.

The old staircase in timber is dressed in mole-coloured sisal. The balustrade is painted and the old stained glass window is restored.

LEFT
The entry hall has a unique feature with its staircase finish in white marble and its internal door in old metal. The budget allocated for the renovation was limited, thus Nathalie Van Reeth decided to conserve the original staircase core. The door is painted, marble is cleaned and the old lamp is conserved.

The rooms at the back of the house are opened to form a large space with an elevated terrace. The large window, custom-made in metal, floods the room in a sea of light. The kitchen is constructed in painted MDF, with the countertop varnished in a darker paint and the floor in white epoxy. The table is custom-made in wenge wood. The timber floor is painted in the same colour.

LEFT
The central area is arranged as a library. The ornaments, parquet floor and the old beveled glass door are conserved and carefully restored.

P.112-113
The wall situated behind the bed forms the structure to the book shelves and lighting partition. The bed is made of tinted oak in the same colour. The bedroom overlooking the dressing room and the bathroom creates an impression of a suite.

The dressing area and the bathroom form a whole. The furniture is finished in the same tinted oak and the old timber floor is sanded down and painted in a darker colour. The countertops are in beige sandstone and the tap fittings are from Vola. This is an atmosphere that breathes serenity, away from the hassle of the city.

A BEAUTIFUL STORY OF THE 1930s

This beautiful building dated 1926, created by architect Herman Van Ooteghem, is situated in an Antwerp district and distinguished by its architectural eclecticism, along with the neoclassical houses to those with pure forms of the Bauhaus.

This house is an almost square construction over the two storeys. It has conserved a superb element of the 1930s: a staircase core in a winding and elegant form.

The rooms are entirely redesigned by the owner to meet his requirement, yet respecting the elements and proportions of the period.

There, we find the obvious contrasts that provide the dynamism to the building: balance between black and white, between the curves of the staircase and rigorously right lines of the room, between the mix and finally between the simple materials and the more sophisticated others.

Left

Contrast is enforced in the entry hall with the white wall and Winkelmans black floor tiles of the period.

Artworks in wood (sculpture of Marc Van de Meulebroek from gallery Faider) and its base made of cord (Christian Astuguevieille) relate to the handrail and the carpet. The vase is from John Pawson, the brushed stainless steel console is from Vanessa De Meulder and the table top is by Adolf Loos. The staircase is covered in sisal for comfort and sonority.

P.118-119

White is presented all over in the house, which contrasts with the other darker tones. The sofas and the brushed stainless steel low tables are designed by Vanessa De Meulder. Here, it is the very colourful African theme that breaks the relationship of black and white.

Silverware by Annick Tapernoux. The linen carpet from Limited Edition laid on the parquet brings warmth to this corner of the living room.

Next

Bookshelves in straight lines made of dark oak and painted MDF is designed by Vanessa De Meulder, as with the custom-made steel open chimney. The timber blinds take the colour of the parquet and let in a soft light from the street. The living room and the dining room are separated by a white cube that delivers a calm note and offers a perfect layout of the space. Chaise longue in black leather by Charles Eames.

The contrast is obtained by placing dark-coloured furniture against the white background. Photo by Marc Luyten opens a new perspective of the back wall. The dark oak table is designed by Vanessa De Meulder. Maxalto chairs in oak and black leather.

LEFT

"Cubex" original kitchen, typical of the period, has a new look due to the new countertop in softened blue stone, the brushed stainless steel door and painted parquet floor. Access to the higher cabinets is made possible by the suspended ladder. "Hello" chairs (Artifort).

LEFT, BOTTOM AND ABOVE

Views of the play in volume of the staircase core, painted entirely in white to accentuate light and its volute. The doors painted in anthracite and tinted parquet floor are in this case a unique touch of contemporary.

Danish chairs from 1950 are covered in white leather. Here, the painting Art & Language adds the unique touch of colour.

LEFT

Bathroom with pure forms finished in Cotto d'Este and oak. Tap fittings from Dornbracht.

LEFT

Intimate ambience as a result of dark walls and cupboards. Soft and subdued lighting from Christian Liaigre. A metal table and a periodic chair. The carpet lines accentuate the depth of the room. Mirrors on the door panels visually enlarge this small room.

P.126-127

In the bedroom, the forms are strict and pure but the draperies (glazed linen for the curtains and velvet of large cotton for the lined bedspread), natural colours and indirect light give the room a subdued and intimate ambience.

CHAPTER III

APARTMENTS, LOFTS AND PENTHOUSES

TO LIVE RATHER THAN RESIDE

Times change, so do values. This is why Obumex launched the challenge to accompany its clients through the styles of different fashions and set the objective to give a form as authentic as possible in a personal experiment of residence.

This urban dwelling, conceived by Kurt Neirynck who is an interior designer at Obumex, constitutes a sublime illustration. Obumex always turns to the most exigent clients and focuses on refinement, elegance, finesse and precision, so that the client can change his or her perception from simply residing to that of living.

P.130-133

All fixtures and niches, chimney, book cabinet, study table and the study cabinets, bedroom cabinets, bathrooms and kitchen are entirely custom-made and painted in harmonious colours with the oak parquet floor. The tones of paint are selected by Obumex. All the furniture comes from Promemoria and Christian Liaigre, with wood and personalised fabrics also assuring a harmonious whole. The carpet and curtains are furnished by Obumex.

P.136-139

The parquet floor and the staircase are in oak: the living areas are in darker tints selected by Obumex while the upper storey is in a brighter finish.

P.140-141

A custom-made work that translates a true passion for perfection.

A TRANSPARENT HOUSE WITH
A VIEW OF GRAZ

In 2001 an old house, situated on the mountainside overhanging the Austrian city of Graz, was torn down to make way for a large modern four-storey dwelling.

On each floor, a large glass bay of window allows wide panoramic views of the old city.

The Dutch decorator Marijke Van Nunen, who also lives in Graz, was commissioned to design an integral interior.

One of the entry halls is entirely painted in bright orange. The floor is finished in Solnhofen natural stone.

LEFT AND ABOVE
The living room is composed of two Casamilano sofas installed symmetrically and a couch from Donghia. The oak parquet is varnished and aged.

NEXT
Total transparency with a view of Graz. The terrace floor is finished in bankirai. The family's object, a sculpture of Mercury on a base support, is placed in the centre of the photo. The curtains are in silk.

The terrace benches are from
Gervasoni.

The tempered glass staircase balustrade reinforces the feel of transparency that generalises the dwelling.

The bookshelves are made of French walnut.
The lounge bench is from Casamilano. The
carpet and coffee table are made-to-measure.

P.150-151

The Bulthaup kitchen combines Nero stainless steel with beech wood. Electrical appliances are from Imperial. The floor is finished in Solnhofen natural stone.

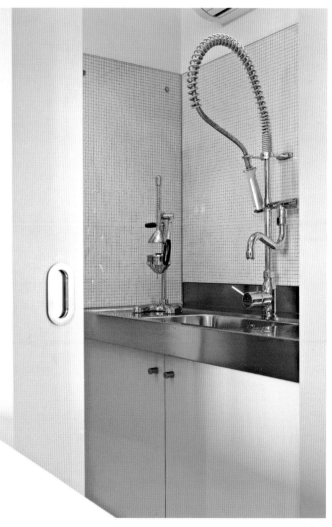

P.152-153

Eight chairs in lilac linen surround the custom-made lacquered table. Above the lacquered console is a tryptic of Cees Roelofs. The small round table was discovered in an antique shop.

On the left is the corridor that leads to the main entry, on the right is a view of the staircase core:
this collection of glass offers an entire view of the four levels of this house.

P.156-157

Similarly, the master bathroom offers a panoramic
view. The floor is a combination of limestone and
wenge wood. Tap fittings are from Dornbracht.

P.158-159

The sauna/relaxation space is finished
in Solnhofen stone.

LEFT

Even the strips of oak parquet for the corridor are bleached and aged.

Two Bonacina in steel and bamboo. The low table is custom-made in bamboo with the structure in wrought iron. On the foreground is a carpet in Manila hemp.

LEFT
The master bedroom. The bedspread and the wall behind the bed are in silk.

The guest bathroom with a basin in grey marble and tinted fir wood.

A STRONG FEEL OF SPACE

Buro Interior sprl was commissioned as the interior designer for this 210-square metre apartment. The architecture of the building was the work of Buro II sprl.

When the client bought the apartment, the plan of the sales agreement showed a subdivision of many small rooms. The client, however, had a specific brief and wanted an apartment that generates a strong sense of space. Thus the interior designer has designed a new subdivision of the apartment.

ABOVE

The long and narrow gas cooker is visually stretched by placing a panel of Oriental Basalt stone on one side and a dark TV niche on the other, both on the same level as the cooker.

OPPOSITE

A lift shaft situated between the living room and the entry, originally an unsightly view, was transformed into a positive element. A base with niches and drawers are arranged into shelving and storing spaces for CDs, books and bar. The base also serves as a separation between the living and entry zones.

LEFT

The 15-metre long living room extends visually into the study room on one end and the master bedroom on the other. The pivoting door on the side of the living area is integrated almost invisibly into the wall.

ABOVE

Bleached oak parquet. "Athos" table from B&B Italia, Zanotta chairs, small side tables from Maxalto. The seats are custom-made.

OPPOSITE

Detail of the kitchen counter. Countertop is in Oriental Basalt, lacquered cabinets and Dornbracht tap fittings.

LEFT

The kitchen partially opens into the living room. The independent kitchen counter situated in front can be closed by a large sliding partition.

The master bedroom with the headboard and bedside tables in bleached oak panels. The finishing of the window edge and the parquet in bleached solid oak are in the same colour as the headboard. The bedroom is adjacent to the living room, the dressing zone and the bathroom. It can be separated from those rooms by sliding doors that disappear entirely into the walls.

LEFT

Washbasins in Oriental Basalt are situated in between the toilets and the cloakroom. The walls around it are painted in the same colour as natural stone.

In the toilets situated next to the entry, the Sanbloc is concealed by narrow furniture in bleached oak. An indirect lighting is integrated on each side of this furniture.

The master bathroom with the floor and wall finished in Oriental Basalt. The lavabo vanity top and bathtub ledge are finished in bleached oak.

A SOBER HARMONY

Buro Interior sprl was commissioned as the interior designer of this 170-square metre apartment. The architecture of the building was the work of Buro II sprl.

Conforming to the client's requirements, the subdivision was radically modified. In light of the apartment's glass bay along the whole length on the front and back, several new layouts are designed to cater to the views. In order to increase the impression of space, the aesthetics is conceived in a sober manner with the choice of materials bringing together a limited and harmonious whole.

ABOVE

The corner salon and the study area are separated by a darker wall with integrated cabinets on the side of the study area. A glass panel that separates the study and the corner dining area gives a view of the whole length of the apartment.

OPPOSITE

The apartment has a large terrace on each side. The table is from Monica Armani and the chairs are from Alias.

LEFT

Armchairs, coffee table and small side tables are from Cassina. Maxalto table and B&B Italia chairs.

OPPOSITE
Bleached parquet is found in all the rooms, interrupted at times by island counters of Pietra Piasentina natural stone.

BELOW
Detail of the Corian countertop that seems to float above the element below that is made of lacquered MDF.

LEFT
The kitchen in a sober conception, with cabinets in lacquered MDF and countertop in white Corian. The electrical appliances are concealed behind a large sliding partition.

"Charles" bed from B&B Italia.

The different rooms that extend visually can be separated by large sliding doors that disappear completely into the cupboard walls when opened. The study table is in white lacquered MDF.

LEFT
The typical white streaks of Pietra Piasentina harmonise perfectly with the Philippe Starck white island bathtub and Carrara marble wall finish.

REFUGE OF AN ART COLLECTOR

Claire Bataille and Paul Ibens have desi-gned an apartment for a passionate mo-dern art collector. The contribution of the lady owner of the house is very important for this project: the numerous collection pieces indeed bring a very personal effect to the final product.

P.176-177

The oak floor is bleached and walls are painted in white. The curtains are in grey silk with beads from Jab. In this space that is reminiscent of a loft, the partitions installed present the artworks similar to an exhibition.

P.178-179

On the left of the photo are two chairs by Christian Liaigre. The chimney is entirely made of Pietra Serena.

On the left of the chimney is a cabinet in iron. On the right is an armchair with white fabric from Axel Vervoordt.

P.180-181

A large panel of Paladino. The raw oak table is a personal design.

The important collection of the owner's artworks is supplemented by its lucky finds. The cabinet with glass shelves is a project of Bataille-Ibens; on the shelf is an antique related to the residence.

A MINIMALIST LOFT IN ANTWERP

The projects of interior designer Filip Deslee can be classified as essentialists, a minimalism that goes beyond simple form. The stake is the search for beauty in the residence. The interiors, small as they are, inspire space and are characterised by their pleasant way of living.

This loft situated in "Ijsfabriek" at Antwerp constitutes an eloquent example of this working manner whereby the key words are mass, volume, lighting, structure and repetition. The whole interior, including the custom-made elements and furniture, is conceived by Filip Deslee.

P.186-187

The walls of the loft are lacquered white and the oak floor is treated to obtain a darker natural colour.

Le Corbusier furniture and lounge couch conceived by Filip Deslee.

Indirect dimmer lighting. The sliding partition of the kitchen is a combination of brown structures and glossed varnished motifs.

NEXT

Tabletop in grey oak. The credence and the cooking stove are finished in rough slate. Countertop is in Corian. Vola tap fittings and "Lem" chairs from La Palma.

P.190-191

A transparent grey tinted glass separates the study area in the bedroom and the shower from the storage area.

The furniture of the bathroom is conceived by Filip Deslee.

The entry hall with a pivot partition in the background is lacquered in fuchsia pink and leads to the toilet.

The bathroom floor is finished in slate.

PHOTOGRAPHY
CREDITS

All the photos: Jo Pauwels, except:

P. 4-5, 40-47, 66-83, 84-101 & 176-185 :   Jean-Luc Laloux
P. 162-169 & 170-175 :   Kris Vandamme